Exploring
Space

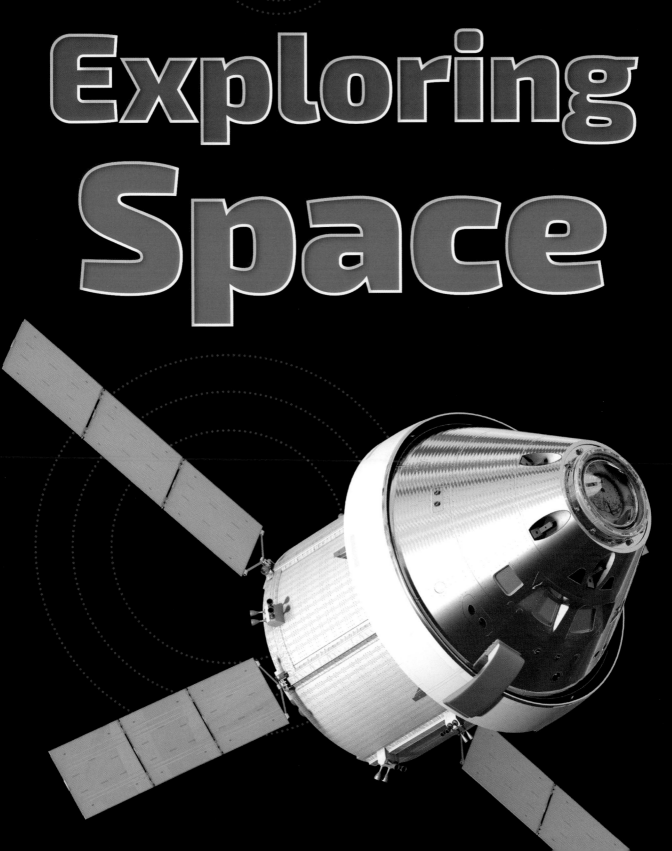

Contents

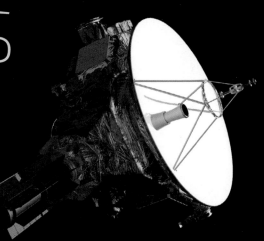

Exploring

Space

If a word is printed **in bold letters that look like this** the first time it appears on any page, you will find the word's meaning in the glossary beginning on page 60.

Astronomers use different kinds of photos to learn about such objects in space as planets. Many photos show an object's natural color. Other photos add false colors or show types of light that the human eye cannot normally see. When appropriate, the captions in this book will state whether a photo uses false color. Other photos and illustrations use color to highlight certain features of interest.

The Awe and Wonder of the Night Sky

Space exploration is our human response to the awe and wonder of the night sky. Since ancient times, people could only look at the heavens from Earth using just their eyes, or through **telescopes.** Beginning in the 1900's, humans gained the ability to leave our home **planet** and venture out into the **solar system** to explore.

Piloted and unpiloted spacecraft venture far beyond the boundaries of Earth to collect valuable information about the solar system and **universe.** Human beings have visited the **moon** and have lived in space stations in **orbit** around Earth for long periods.

Such exploration helps us see Earth in its true relation with the rest of the universe.

Where Space Begins

There is no clear boundary between the **atmosphere** of Earth and outer space. The farther you go from Earth's surface, the thinner the air gets. But most scientists say that outer space begins about 60 miles (95 kilometers) above Earth. Most scientists view the **Karman Line**, an imaginary boundary about 62 miles (100 kilometers) above Earth's surface, as the **start of outer space.**

The Karman Line marks the boundary between Earth's atmosphere and outer space.

Karman Line

Space **Probes**

The era of human space exploration is still very young. Humans have not yet managed to send people beyond Earth's moon. Even the most powerful telescopes on Earth can only provide a fuzzy image of Pluto and other remote objects in our solar system. Yet scientists have vastly expanded our view of the solar system with missions using unpiloted space **probes.**

A space probe is an unpiloted craft launched into space to gather *data* (information) that is radioed back to Earth. Some probes gather samples of material from a distant object. Such a probe may return the samples to Earth, or it may *analyze* (determine the nature of) the samples and radio back the results.

Space probes have visited every planet in our solar system. Some have journeyed beyond the planets. Others have traveled—or continue to travel—in orbit around a planet or the sun. A few have even orbited **asteroids** and **comets.**

Some probes have even landed on planets, moons, and other space objects. A probe that crash lands is called an *impact vehicle,* or *impactor.* A **lander** performs experiments and records data after coming to rest on the surface of an object. A special kind of lander, called a **rover,** can move under its own power to explore the surface of the object.

This illustration shows the spacecraft Cassini in front of the Milky Way, our home galaxy.

Space Probes

Do What Astronauts Cannot

A spacecraft must reach a speed of about 25,000 miles (40,000 kilometers) per hour to escape **Earth's gravity.**

Sending people to explore the solar system is hard. Overcoming Earth's **gravity** is a spacecraft's **biggest challenge.** A powerful **rocket** called a **launch vehicle** helps a spacecraft overcome gravity and reach space.

Human space exploration has **many dangers.** Tragic accidents have taken the lives of United States **astronauts** as well as **cosmonauts** in the Soviet space program. Long missions mean people have to eat, sleep, and live in a spacecraft.

The MAVEN space probe, launched in 2013, was designed to study the Martian atmosphere while orbiting Mars.

Probes can visit

uncharted regions

of space or patrol familiar regions to collect data over a long time. But in some cases, people must follow the probes and use human ingenuity, flexibility, and courage to explore the mysteries of the universe.

Space probes have many advantages over piloted missions. Unpiloted probes are cheaper, smaller, safer, and faster than piloted vehicles. Probes can make trips that would be too risky for human beings to attempt. Probes can study hostile and dangerous places where human beings

could never survive.

Venturing
Out

The first space probes launched from Earth were sent to the moon, our planet's closest neighbor. The Soviet Union was the first country to launch a space probe. It was called Luna 1. In 1959, Luna 1 passed within about 3,700 miles (6,000 kilometers) of the moon.

FUN FACT

Vanguard I, the first **satellite** successfully launched by the United States, has been

orbiting Earth
since 1958.

Some of the satellite's data proved that Earth is not perfectly round. This information has helped mapmakers make more accurate world maps.

Soon after, in March 1959, the United States National Aeronautics and Space Administration (NASA) launched the Pioneer 4 probe that flew by the moon. Six months later, the Soviet Union's Luna 2 became the first probe to hit the moon. Luna 3 photographed the moon's far side that is always turned away from Earth.

In 1964 and 1965, three U.S. Ranger spacecraft took the first close-up television pictures of the moon before crashing into the surface. In 1966, the Soviet Union's Luna 9 became the first probe to touch down gently on the moon.

Beginning in 1965, NASA launched a series of Pioneer probes into orbit around the sun. Several of these probes operated for more than 20 years. NASA also sent a series of landers, named Surveyor, to the moon. Surveyor 1 sent thousands of images of the moon's surface back to Earth.

This illustration shows the Luna 1, the first space probe. In 1959, it passed by the moon.

The First Piloted
Spacecraft

The very first piloted spacecraft, the Soviet Union's Vostok, had room for only one person. On April 12, 1961, Yuri Gagarin *(gah GAHR ihn)* became the first person to travel into space on Vostok 1. Vostok was designed to land on the ground. The first piloted spacecraft designed by the United States—called Mercury—was designed to land in the ocean.

The first American in space was Alan B. Shepard, Jr. On May 5, 1961, he flew 117 miles (188 kilometers) into space on a Mercury rocket called Freedom 7. He landed safely back on Earth 15 minutes later.

Later astronaut **capsules** were made bigger so that two or more people could travel on a flight. These capsules were also able to carry more supplies so that astronauts could stay in space longer. The first spacecraft could stay in space for less than a day. But soon spacecraft could remain in space for up to two weeks.

FUN FACT

Spacecraft have sometimes been changed because of comments from the astronauts or experiences during testing and flight. For example, astronauts asked for **a larger window** on an early Mercury capsule, and NASA designed one.

The Soviet Union's Vostok was the first piloted spacecraft. It carried the first person into space in April 1961.

Walking on the
Moon

In less than a decade,

humans went from building rockets that could barely reach space to setting foot on the moon. The United States space program to reach the moon was called Apollo. The program lasted from 1961 to 1975.

Apollo's rocket,

the Saturn V, had to produce enough power to propel astronauts on the roughly 250,000-mile (400,000-kilometer) journey from Earth to the moon. The rocket measured taller than a 30-story building.

Astronaut Neil A. Armstrong, commanding the Apollo 11 mission, was the first person to walk on the surface of the moon. After taking the first step on its barren landscape on July 20, 1969, he spoke the now-famous words, "That's one small step for a man,

one giant leap

for mankind."

Astronaut Buzz Aldrin walks on the surface of the moon near a leg of the Apollo 11 lunar module on July 20, 1969.

Earth's moon is the only place in the solar system beyond Earth where humans have set foot. In six successful missions, 12 people in the Apollo program

walked on the moon.

Human space exploration

largely ended with the Apollo program. In the following years, scientists launched several bold missions to explore the solar system using unpiloted space probes.

Space Probes to
Venus and Mercury

Even as the Apollo program was going on, scientists were launching probes to explore the planets of the solar system. Venus and Mercury, the two innermost planets of the solar system, were among the first to be visited.

Americans launched successful probes to conduct flybys of Venus in 1962, 1967, and 1974. But the first probe to actually land on Venus was the Soviet Union's Venera 7. It touched down in 1970, becoming the first probe to land on another planet.

In 1978, NASA sent two probes to Venus, Pioneer Venus 1 and 2. These probes recorded valuable data on the planet's atmosphere. The Soviet probe Venera 8 landed on Venus in 1982. It survived for more than two hours in the heat and crushing atmosphere. Venera 8 sent the first color photographs of the surface of Venus back to Earth.

NASA's Mariner 10 was the first spacecraft to reach Mercury. It flew to within 460 miles (740 kilometers) of the planet in 1974. It took close-up pictures of the planet's moonlike surface. No other probes were sent to Mercury until 2008.

This illustration shows the Soviet Venera 13 probe on Venus. It landed on the planet in 1982. The probe transmitted photographs of the planet's surface.

Destination
Mars!

Humans have launched more missions of exploration to Mars compared with any other planet in our solar system. The first space probe to visit the red planet, called Mariner 4, flew past in 1965. However, not all of the missions to Mars have been successful.

In 1971, the Soviet Mars 2 lander crashed to the surface of Mars. Days later, Mars 3 completed the first successful soft landing on Mars. The probe transmitted for 20 seconds before its controllers lost contact. Following close behind, NASA's Mariner 9 went into orbit around Mars in 1971. It took images of the planet and mapped most of Mars.

The busiest probes on Mars in the 1970's were NASA's Viking 1 and Viking 2. Both probes landed on Mars in 1976. They took pictures and issued Martian weather reports for several years.

Viking 1's robot arm scooped up a bit of Martian sediment. It dropped the sample into a special onboard laboratory to test for evidence of **microbes.** The experiment discovered a lot of chemical activity in the sediment, but provided no clear evidence for life on Mars.

Space Pioneers

Early space probes from Earth visited the nearby inner planets of the solar system: Mercury, Venus, and Mars. Sending probes to explore the outer regions of our solar system presented more of a challenge to scientists.

Probes to Jupiter and beyond must travel across vast distances of space. Radio commands from Earth to robotic probes take hours to transmit. **Radiation** in space destroys camera lenses, and computer circuits must be shielded from it to prevent damage.

The first probes to travel as far as Jupiter were NASA's Pioneer 10 in 1973 and Pioneer 11 in 1974. The probes made the journey through the solar system's main asteroid belt and took the first close-up images of Jupiter.

After its Jupiter flyby, Pioneer 11 headed for Saturn and sent back stunning images of the planet. The missions ended in the mid-1990's as the probes ran out of fuel. But both probes are still flying away from the planets and towards **interstellar** space (the space between the stars).

Is Anyone Out There?

As they leave our solar system for outer space, the Pioneer probes each carry a golden plaque with a message to any intelligent life that may find them. The plaque includes a greeting, a simple map showing Earth's location, and a drawing of a man and a woman.

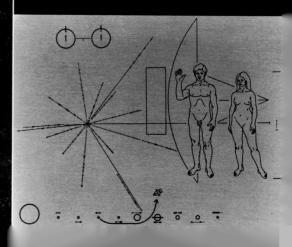

This illustration shows the Pioneer 10 as it passes by Jupiter in December 1973. It was the first probe to pass through an asteroid belt. It was also the first spacecraft to send back detailed images of Jupiter and its moons.

The **Voyager** Probes

Sun

Voyager 1

Jupiter

Saturn

Uranus

Both probes passed by and photographed Jupiter and Saturn. Voyager 1 also studied Titan, Saturn's moon. This detour to Titan led Voyager 1 on a path away from the planets of the solar system.

No space probe has visited more planets than the NASA **Voyager** missions. These probes were launched on missions of solar system exploration on a grand scale not seen before.

NASA launched Voyager 1 and Voyager 2 in 1977. The two probes were designed to last for five years, while making flybys of the planets Jupiter and Saturn. But the probes **performed so well** that NASA scientists extended their missions.

With its
mission extended,

Voyager 2 was the first space probe to visit Uranus *(YUR uh nuhs),* in 1986, and Neptune, in 1989. The probe photographed clouds on Uranus and a huge storm on Neptune. The Voyagers discovered almost two dozen moons in orbit around the outer planets.

In 2012, Voyager 1 became the first human-made craft to enter

interstellar space.

Voyager 2 reached interstellar space on a different path in 2018.

FUN FACT

Voyager 2 was launched in August 1977

before

Voyager 1 (launched in September). Mission controllers did this so the probes could take different paths on different schedules in case one probe failed. Voyager 1 arrived at Jupiter first.

Voyager 2

Neptune

This diagram shows the paths taken by the Voyager 1 (orange track) and Voyager 2 (red track) spacecraft.

Voyager 2's Grand Tour

When the Voyager spacecraft were launched separately in 1977, NASA mission controllers left nothing to chance. Both twin probes carried the same instruments. If one probe failed, the hope was that the other would complete the mission. As planned, both probes arrived near Jupiter in 1979 and went on to fly by Saturn.

NASA mission controllers also knew that they could take advantage of a rare event to extend the Voyager 2 mission. At the time, Jupiter, Saturn, Uranus, and Neptune were lined up in space in an arrangement that occurs only once every 175 years. They radioed instructions that enabled Voyager 2 to continue towards Uranus and Neptune.

Voyager 2 made a close flyby of Uranus in 1986 and reached Neptune in 1989. It sent incredible images of these distant worlds back to Earth. Visiting the four outermost planets of the solar system, NASA dubbed the Voyager 2 extended mission the "Grand Tour" of the solar system.

Today, both Voyager 1 and Voyager 2 are still traveling into interstellar space. Voyager 2 still sends information from the edge of the solar system.

This illustration shows the Voyager 2 probe as it leaves our solar system and heads into interstellar space.

FUN FACT

Gravity assists

were first used with probes to the moon and inner planets.

Sun

Ear

This illustration shows Voyager 2 as it slingshots around Jupiter in a gravity assist toward Saturn, Uranus, and Neptune.

Jupiter

Gravity
Assist

What was so special about the alignment of Jupiter, Saturn, Uranus, and Neptune? It allowed the Voyager probes to "slingshot" through the solar system at high speed, visiting several targets in a short period of time.

The rockets that launched the Voyager probes were among the most powerful ever built. But it would have taken 30 years for them to get a probe like Voyager directly from Earth to Uranus, and even longer for Neptune.

NASA controllers set the Voyager probes to fly past Jupiter at a special angle. As each spacecraft approached Jupiter, the planet's powerful gravity flung the Voyager craft past and off towards Saturn at higher speeds than they started with. Such a maneuver is called a *gravity assist.*

Mission controllers maneuvered Voyager 1 to fly past Saturn's moon Titan. This put Voyager 1 on a path out of the solar system. But Voyager 2 used a gravity assist from Saturn to get to Uranus and then, with another assist, to Neptune. The probe took just 12 years to complete the Grand Tour of the outer solar system.

Mars

Voyager 2

Return to
Mars

As scientists developed better space probes, they launched new missions of exploration to Mars, Earth's most interesting neighbor.

In 1996, NASA launched the Mars Global Surveyor to map the surface of Mars. The orbiting probe's camera recorded images that suggested water may once have existed on Mars. In 2001, NASA launched the Mars Odyssey. In 2002, this probe discovered vast amounts of **water ice** just below the Martian surface.

In 2003, the European Space Agency (ESA) launched the Mars Express. This probe took pictures of the Martian surface and

This illustration shows the Mars InSight lander on the surface of Mars in 2018. The lander's instruments will record data on the crust and interior of Mars.

the icecap covering the planet's southernmost region. It also detected **methane** in the Martian atmosphere. On Earth, methane is produced by living things as well as by nonliving processes. NASA's Mars Reconnaissance Orbiter began orbiting Mars in 2006. In 2015, the craft found evidence that liquid water flows just below the Martian surface during warm seasons.

In 2018, the U.S. InSight lander touched down on Mars. InSight stands for *In*terior Exploration using *S*eismic *I*nvestigations, *G*eodesy, and *H*eat *T*ransport. The lander's instruments will record data on the crust and interior of Mars to help answer questions about how the planet formed.

Mars Rovers

Most of what we now know about Mars has come from

landers and rovers.

These missions have discovered evidence that Mars once had water on its surface and may have even had life.

NASA's Pathfinder probe landed on Mars in 1997. The probe carried a rover about the size of

a toy wagon.

In three months, the rover—called Sojourner—traveled a little over 100 yards (91 meters).

Sojourner analyzed the Martian sediment and rocks and passed its data to Pathfinder. Pathfinder radioed the data to NASA scientists on Earth. The scientists

steered Sojourner

using radio signals. Sojourner also used sensors to avoid obstacles.

The Pathfinder probe and Sojourner rover are shown on the surface of Mars in this color-enhanced image. The Pathfinder landed on Mars in 1997.

In 2004, NASA landed two more rovers—named Spirit and Opportunity—in different areas of Mars. Opportunity discovered surprising **minerals.** On Earth, these minerals are found only in rocks formed in water or exposed to it. NASA scientists concluded

that liquid water

may have covered the area. Spirit also discovered minerals often found with water.

In 2005, Opportunity ran across a **meteorite.** It was the

first meteorite

found on any planet other than Earth. Spirit functioned until 2010. Opportunity continued to operate until it was knocked out by a dust storm in 2018.

Phoenix and Curiosity

Discoveries on Mars

In August 2007, NASA launched the Phoenix lander to Mars to search for direct evidence of water ice in the Martian soil. Phoenix parachuted to a landing on Mars's northern plains in June 2008.

Phoenix had a robot arm with an "elbow" that could dig beneath the Martian surface. NASA scientists on Earth used the arm to scoop up some sediment and deliver it to instruments aboard the lander. Data from the instruments provided the first direct evidence of water ice on Mars. The data also showed that liquid water once flowed on the planet's surface.

Curiosity, the largest probe to land on another planet or moon, arrived on Mars in August 2012. It discovered further evidence that liquid water once flowed across the Martian surface. Curiosity also found clear evidence that Mars could have once hosted life.

This illustration shows the Curiosity rover examining a rock on Mars with a set of tools at the end of the rover arm. It arrived on Mars in August 2012.

New **Lunar Probes**

This illustration shows the twin spacecraft, Ebb and Flow, that make up the NASA GRAIL mission. In 2012, the pair detailed observations of the moon's gravitational field from lunar orbit.

Since the mid-1990's, the United States and other nations have returned to the moon with probes to explore and learn about the surface. In 1994, the U.S. orbiter Clementine conducted a four-month mission observing the moon. It first detected evidence of water ice on the moon surface. The U.S. probe Lunar Prospector circled the moon from 1998 to 1999 and also found indications of water ice.

ESA launched the SMART-1 spacecraft that orbited the moon from 2004 to 2006. It studied the moon's chemical composition. Japan's SELENE spacecraft and China's first moon probe, Chang'e 1, both orbited the moon from 2007 to 2009. These probes also studied chemical elements in the moon.

India launched its Chandrayaan-1 mission in 2008. The craft entered lunar orbit and mapped the moon's surface. The spacecraft also released a probe meant to crash on the surface and eject debris that could be analyzed from afar for the presence of water.

In June 2009, NASA launched the Lunar Reconnaissance Orbiter (LRO). The LRO orbited the moon, creating three-dimensional maps of its surface. In 2011, NASA launched the twin satellites of the GRAIL mission. The pair detailed observations of the moon's gravitational field from lunar orbit in 2012.

In 2019, China landed its Chang'e 4 probe on the moon's far side. A satellite, launched in 2018, orbits the moon and relays data between Earth and the Chang'e 4 lander.

More
Jupiter Probes

In 1989, NASA sent a spacecraft called Galileo to Jupiter. Arriving in 1995, Galileo was the first probe to orbit one of the outer planets of the solar system. Galileo orbited Jupiter for eight years.

Galileo was a two-part probe. The larger probe released a small probe into Jupiter's atmosphere. The small probe collected data for about an hour before it was crushed in Jupiter's dense atmosphere. Meanwhile, the larger probe orbited the planet and observed Jupiter's larger moons. It found evidence that an ocean of water may lie beneath the icy surface of Europa, one of Jupiter's larger moons. In 2003, as fuel ran out, Galileo was intentionally crashed into Jupiter, ending the mission.

In 2007, NASA's New Horizons spacecraft flew past Jupiter on its way to Pluto and beyond. In that short visit, New Horizons photographed lightning near Jupiter's poles.

In 2011, NASA launched the probe Juno to Jupiter. It began orbiting the planet in 2016. Juno will study the planet to learn more about its composition and formation.

The probe Juno is shown orbiting the planet Jupiter in this illustration. Launched in 2011, the probe began orbiting the planet in 2016.

Cassini at
Saturn

In 1997, NASA launched a probe called Cassini. The spacecraft included a smaller probe called Huygens *(HOY gehns),* built by ESA. Cassini-Huygens's job was to study Saturn, its rings, and its larger moons.

Cassini entered Saturn's orbit in 2004. On December 25, Cassini released Huygens. The small probe parachuted through the smoggy atmosphere of Saturn's moon Titan. For 2 ½ hours, the probe analyzed chemicals, recorded sounds, and measured wind speeds as it floated to the moon's surface. It also shot pictures of what looked like lakes and riverbeds on Titan's surface before landing on a wet surface of sandlike grains of ice.

This illustration shows the Huygens probe parachuting through the atmosphere of Saturn's moon Titan. Cassini released the probe on Dec. 25, 2004.

Meanwhile, the Cassini spacecraft observed Saturn's rings. In 2006, images showed gaps in one of the outer rings. The gaps seemed to have been made by small bodies called "moonlets." The moonlets support a theory that Saturn's rings formed from a larger, moon-sized body that broke apart.

By 2017, Cassini's fuel supply was almost exhausted. Mission controllers programmed Cassini to destroy itself in September 2017 by crashing into Saturn's atmosphere. They did this so that the probe could not crash into any of Saturn's moons.

This illustration shows the Cassini spacecraft in front of the planet Saturn. The probe entered Saturn's orbit in 2004.

New
Horizons

Since its discovery in 1930, **astronomers** could only study Pluto as a dim, grainy blur in photographs taken by Earth-based or orbiting telescopes. But that all changed with NASA's New Horizons mission, launched in 2006.

The New Horizons probe flew by Pluto in 2015. The main goal of the mission was to explore Pluto and its large moon Charon. For the first time, astronomers could see sharp, close-up images of this distant world.

New Horizons continued on to explore the **Kuiper belt,** a band of icy bodies largely beyond the orbit of Neptune.

This illustration shows the New Horizons spacecraft in front of the dwarf planet Pluto. The probe flew by Pluto in 2015.

Arrokoth

In 2019, the New Horizons probe flew past and made a close observation of 2014 MU69, a small Kuiper belt object (KBO) that scientists named Arrokoth. The KBO is less than 30 miles (45 kilometers) in **diameter**, and its orbit lies about 1 billion miles (1.5 billion kilometers) beyond that of Pluto.

Arrokoth is the

most distant object
ever observed directly by a space probe launched from Earth.

Solar Probes

The **first spacecraft** used to study the sun were rockets launched above Earth's atmosphere in the 1940's. The rockets gathered information about X rays and **ultraviolet rays** from the sun.

In the 1960's, astronomers used satellites to study the **solar wind** (particles streaming from the sun).

NASA and ESA launched a probe called Ulysses from the space shuttle Discovery in 1990. Ulysses became the first probe to orbit the sun's **polar regions.**

ESA's Solar and Heliospheric Observatory (SOHO), launched in 1995, studied the **sun's interior,** its atmosphere, and the solar wind.

In 2001, NASA's Genesis spacecraft gathered samples of the solar wind. **Genesis crashed** when it returned to Earth in 2004. Still, scientists were able to save some of the samples.

In 2006, Japan's Hinode and NASA's STEREO spacecraft began gathering information about eruptions from the sun and the sun's magnetic field. STEREO is **a pair of space observatories.** STEREO stands for Solar *TE*rrestrial *RE*lations *O*bservatory. In 2015, the STEREO probes crossed paths on the far side of the sun.

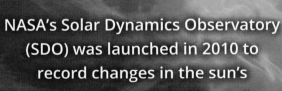
FUN FACT

NASA's Solar Dynamics Observatory (SDO) was launched in 2010 to record changes in the sun's **magnetic field** in greater detail than ever before.

Touching the Sun

In 2018, NASA launched the Parker Solar Probe. This spacecraft will fly to within 3.9 million miles (6.2 million kilometers) of the sun's surface. That's close enough to enter the sun's outer atmosphere!

The probe has four instruments designed to study solar wind in detail. At closest approach to the sun, the portion of the probe facing the sun will heat up to about 2550 °F (1400 °C). But the inside of the probe will remain at about room temperature!

During its mission, the Parker Solar Probe will use seven gravity assists around Venus to increase speed.

At closest approach, the Parker Solar Probe will be orbiting around the sun at nearly 430,000 miles (692,017 kilometers) per hour! That's fast enough to travel around the world in about 3 ½ minutes! No craft ever launched by humans has traveled so fast.

This illustration shows the Parker Solar Probe observing the sun. The probe was launched in 2018.

Probing
Comets

Exploring the solar system is not limited to observing planets and moons. Scientists are also interested in comets. These balls of ice and dust are thought to be left over from the formation of the outer planets.

In 2004, NASA's Stardust probe flew by Comet Wild 2 and collected samples of the dust and gas surrounding the comet's **core.** The Stardust samples revealed material that had formed closer to the sun, rather than the outer planets.

In 2005, NASA launched the Deep Impact spacecraft to Comet Tempel 1 as it neared the sun. The craft consisted of two probes: an impactor and a *flyby craft.* In July, the impactor probe hit the comet and created a large **crater.** The impactor took pictures of the comet before smashing into it. The larger, flyby probe took pictures of the crash as it happened. The crash helped reveal what kind of material made up the comet.

In 2010, NASA used Deep Impact, renamed EPOXI, to explore Comet Hartley 2. In 2011, the Stardust-NExT space probe mission flew within about 100 miles (160 kilometers) of Tempel 1. Stardust photographed the spot on the comet where the Deep Impact probe collided with it in 2005.

In 2014, ESA's Rosetta probe went into orbit around the comet 67P/Churyumov-Gerasimenko. Rosetta released a small lander called Philae that touched down on the comet's surface. Rosetta sent back images of the comet seconds before a planned collision into the comet ended its mission in 2016.

This illustration shows ESA's Rosetta probe (far left) and the Philae lander above the comet 67P/Churyumov-Gerasimenko.

Probes to
Asteroids

The solar system is not just planets. There are millions of smaller bodies, called asteroids, in orbit around our sun. Scientists want to study asteroids because they are made up of the leftover material from the formation of the solar system. They can provide information on how the solar system formed.

NASA's Near Earth Asteroid Rendezvous (NEAR) probe studied the asteroids Mathilde in 1997 and Eros in 2000. In 2007, NASA launched the Dawn probe to study Vesta and Ceres, the two largest objects in the **main asteroid belt.** Dawn mapped the surface of Vesta in 2012 and Ceres in 2015.

In 2005, Japan's Hayabusa probe visited an asteroid called Itokawa. Despite the failure of several of its systems, the craft transmitted detailed pictures of the asteroid and landed on its surface. In 2010, Hayabusa returned samples of the surface material to Earth for analysis.

In 2014, Japan launched the Hayabusa2 spacecraft. In 2019, the probe touched down on its target asteroid, called Ryugu, about 1.9 billion miles (3 billion kilometers) from Earth.

Hayabusa2 collected samples of the asteroid and will return them to Earth for study by the end of 2020.

Returning Humans to Space

Exploration of our solar system using piloted spacecraft largely ended once the last Apollo mission left the moon. However, new missions to send humans back to the moon and even to Mars are now being planned. These missions must overcome many challenges to enable people to live and work safely in space.

Spacecraft that carry astronauts must provide everything people need to survive. They must provide the astronauts with water to drink and air to breathe. Meals on spacecraft must be easy to make and store.

Spacecraft also have heating and cooling controls to keep the temperature comfortable. Special toilets on board suck body wastes into collection containers. Trash is kept in unused places on the space vehicle. It is thrown overboard or brought back to Earth.

Astronauts wash themselves with wet towels. Some space stations have showers. Space travelers have special sleeping bags strapped to a cushion and a pillow. However, most astronauts like to sleep floating in the air. They just wear a few straps to keep them from bouncing around the cabin. Some astronauts wear blindfolds to block the sunlight that streams in the windows.

NASA's Orion spacecraft is designed to take human explorers farther into space than any previous craft.

NASA astronaut Karen Nyberg looks at Earth through a window aboard the ISS.

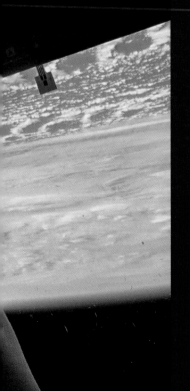

Microgravity
and Space Travel

Astronauts are frequently shown floating aboard a spacecraft in what is often called "zero gravity" or weightlessness. Zero gravity is actually **microgravity,** a state of extremely low gravity. During space flights, microgravity affects both astronauts and their spacecraft.

Microgravity affects the human body in many ways. In the first few days of a mission, about half of all space travelers experience "space sickness." Travelers feel confused—like they are always upside down, no matter which way they turn. They may become sick and vomit. Other effects on the body include a muscle weakness known as deconditioning.

Microgravity affects a spacecraft just as much as it does the astronauts. In a microgravity environment, fuel does not drain from tanks, so it must be squeezed out by high-pressure gas. Hot air does not rise in microgravity, so fans must be used to circulate the air.

In space, astronauts can eat upside down—or at least **upside down** in relation to the spacecraft. That is because in space, there is no true "up" or "down"!

NASA astronaut Scott Kelly gives himself a flu shot aboard the ISS for a study on the human immune system.

Effects of Space Travel on the
Human Body

A piloted mission to Mars means astronauts must live for months in microgravity. Before such missions can be launched, scientists need to understand the long-term effects such conditions have on the human body.

American astronaut Scott Kelly spent a yearlong mission living in microgravity aboard the International Space Station (ISS), from 2015 to 2016. NASA scientists were interested in the changes that took place in Kelly's body while he was in space.

Scott Kelly's identical twin brother, fellow astronaut Mark Kelly, remained on Earth during the mission. NASA scientists could then compare him with his brother after a year in space. They found that Scott had become about 2 inches (5 centimeters) taller in space, and his overall body mass had decreased. Once he returned to Earth, however, Scott's body soon returned to its usual size.

NASA scientists also found that Scott Kelly's bone growth, immune system, and eyesight had altered function after a year in space when compared with Mark's. Many of the changes they observed in Scott Kelly appeared to be permanent.

NASA astronauts Eric Boe and Suni Williams (inset right) wear Boeing's new space suit designed to be worn by astronauts flying on the CST-100 Starliner capsule.

Suiting Up

An astronaut wears a special space suit while on a mission. The suit has many layers of material. It keeps the astronaut from getting too hot or cold. For spacewalks, equipment in a backpack supplies the astronaut with air to breathe. A helmet blocks out strong, harmful rays from the sun. Thin, flexible gloves allow the astronaut to feel small objects and handle tools. The astronaut communicates with the crew and mission control through a radio.

In 2017, the American company Boeing, one of the world's largest manufacturers of aerospace equipment, unveiled a new space suit design that astronauts will wear aboard the company's Starliner capsule. The capsule will travel to and from low-Earth orbit destinations, such as the ISS. The bright blue space suit is smaller and lighter and will keep an astronaut cooler.

The suit has touchscreen-sensitive gloves to allow the astronauts to interact with the capsule's tablets. A communications headset helps connect astronauts to ground and space crews. Boots designed like cross-training sport shoes are breathable and slip-resistant.

To the Moon
and Beyond

In the early 2000's, NASA began developing Orion, a capsule-shaped spacecraft designed to take human explorers farther into space than any previous craft. The spacecraft is planned to carry astronauts to the ISS in orbit around Earth and, eventually, to the moon and Mars.

Orion is designed to sustain astronauts during a long mission into deep space and return them safely to Earth. Astronauts will be carried in Orion's Crew Exploration Vehicle (CEV). The Orion CEV will be launched into space using a powerful new heavy-lift rocket called the Space Launch System (SLS).

The first successful unpiloted test flight of the Orion spacecraft took place in 2014. It was launched aboard a Delta IV rocket. Orion missions with astronauts are expected to take place in the 2020's. The lunar exploration program, called Artemis, aims to use Orion to land the first woman and the next man on the moon.

This illustration shows the SLS taking off from Earth. The SLS will be the most powerful rocket ever built for planned space missions to Mars.

Glossary

asteroid A small body made of rocky material or metal that orbits a star.

astronaut A pilot or member of the crew of a spacecraft.

astronomer A scientist who studies stars, planets, and other objects or forces in space.

atmosphere *(AT muh sfihr)* The mass of gases that surrounds a planet or other body.

capsule A section of a spacecraft that can be used or ejected as a unit.

comet A small body made of dirt and ice that orbits the sun.

core The center part of the inside of a planet, moon, or star.

cosmonaut A Russian astronaut.

crater A bowl-shaped depression on the surface of a planet or other body created by the impact of an object.

diameter The length of a straight line through the middle of a circle or anything shaped like a ball.

gravity The force of attraction that acts between all objects because of their mass.

interstellar Situated or taking place between the stars.

Karman line An altitude of about 62 miles (100 kilometers) above Earth's surface (from sea level). This height has become an international boundary marking the beginning of outer space.

Kuiper *(KY pur)* **belt** A ring of icy objects orbiting in the outer solar system beyond Neptune. Scientists believe that many comets are objects from the Kuiper belt.

lander A spacecraft designed for landing instead of orbiting; landing vehicle.

launch vehicle A rocket that carries a satellite or spacecraft into space.

main asteroid belt The region between Mars and Jupiter where most asteroids exist.

meteorite A mass of stone or metal from outer space that has reached the surface of a planet or moon without burning up in that body's atmosphere.

methane A compound formed of the chemical elements carbon and hydrogen.

microbe A living organism so small that a microscope is needed to see it.

microgravity A condition of very low gravity, especially approaching weightlessness.

mineral A substance, such as tin, salt, or sulfur, that is formed naturally in rocks.

moon A smaller body that orbits a planet or other body.

orbit The path that a smaller body takes around a larger body; for instance, the path that a planet takes around the sun.

planet A large, round body in space that orbits a star. A planet must have sufficient gravitational pull to clear other objects from the area of its orbit.

probe An unpiloted device sent to explore space. Most probes send *data* (information) from space back to Earth.

radiation Energy given off in the form of waves or small particles of matter.

rocket A type of engine that pushes itself forward or upward by producing *thrust* (a force).

rover A robotic device that can move about, explore, and collect information under its own power via remote control.

satellite An artificial or natural object in space that revolves around another object, such as a planet. Humans launch artificial satellites for communication or to study Earth and other objects in space. A moon is a natural satellite that orbits a planet or other large body in space.

solar system A group of bodies in space made up of a star and the planets and other objects orbiting around that star.

telescope An instrument for making distant objects appear nearer and larger. Simple telescopes usually consist of an arrangement of lenses, and sometimes mirrors, in one or more tubes.

ultraviolet rays An invisible form of light. The sun is the major natural source of ultraviolet rays on Earth.

universe Everything that exists anywhere in space and time.

water ice A term scientists use to describe frozen water, to distinguish it from ice that forms from other chemical substances.

Index

World Book, Inc.
180 North LaSalle Street
Suite 900
Chicago, Illinois 60601
USA

For information about other "Solar System" titles, as well as other World Book print and digital publications, please go to www.worldbook.com or call 1-800-WORLDBK (967-5325).

For information about sales to schools and libraries, call 1-800-975-3250 (United States) or 1-800-837-5365 (Canada).

Library of Congress Cataloging-in-Publication Data for this volume has been applied for.

Our Solar System
ISBN: 978-0-7166-8058-1 (set, hc.)

Exploring Space
ISBN: 978-0-7166-8068-0 (hc.)

Also available as:
ISBN: 978-0-7166-8078-9 (e-book)

Printed in the United States of America
by CG Book Printers,
North Mankato, Minnesota
1st printing March 2020

Staff

Editorial

Writer
Shawn Brennan

Manager, New Product
Nicholas Kilzer

Editors
Will Adams
Mellonee Carrigan

Proofreader
Nathalie Strassheim

Manager, Indexing Services
David Pofelski

Graphics and Design

Senior Visual Communications Designer
Melanie Bender

Media Editor
Rosalia Bledsoe

Manufacturing/Production

Manufacturing Manager
Anne Fritzinger

Production Specialist
Curley Hunter

Acknowledgments

Cover: © Nuttawut Uttamaharad, Shutterstock; NASA Orion Spacecraft
1   NASA Orion Spacecraft
2-3   NASA/JPL-Caltech; NASA/Johns Hopkins University Applied Physics Laboratory/ Southwest Research Institute; NASA Orion Spacecraft
4-9   © Shutterstock
10-11 © Detlev van Ravenswaay, Science Source
12-13 © Mechanik/Shutterstock
14-15 NASA
16-17 © Raymond Cassel, Shutterstock
18-21 NASA
22-23 © Julian Baum, Science Source
24-25 © Mark Garlick, Science Source; NASA

26-27 © David A. Hardy, Science Source/Getty Images
28-35 NASA/JPL
36-37 © Naeblys/Shutterstock
38-39 © Dotted Yeti/Shutterstock; D. Ducros/ESA/ NASA
40-41 © Dotted Yeti/Shutterstock; NASA/Johns Hopkins University Applied Physics Laboratory/ Southwest Research Institute/Roman Tkachenko
42-43 © Skorzewiak/Shutterstock
44-45 NASA
46-47 ESA/Rosetta/NavCam
48-49 © Walter Myers, Stocktrek Images/Getty Images
50-59 NASA